THE ELITE

Principles to save your Hard Earned Money

GROCERY

SHOPPER

Raymond Reitano

Outskirts Press, Inc.
Denver, Colorado

Acknowledgements

I dedicate this book to the God of my creation, my king Jesus Christ, and to my family. I thank them for their support over the years.

I also dedicate this book to all the people who will benefit from the knowledge that has been given to me over the 30 years that I've been working on these principles.

CONTENTS

INTRODUCTION

There is a grocery shopper walking up and down the aisles with a shopping trolley full of items, looking around, buying food, and making decisions about dinner on the fly. This person doesn't have a list, and is frantically thinking about everything that is needed for the week to come. This shopper is not really looking at anything but the obvious savings that have been posted by the store, and is continually returning to the same aisles, going back and forth because of forgotten items or last-minute decisions. Have you ever seen a shopper like this? Perhaps you recognize yourself? We have all seen people like this in our local store.

This shopper is going into battle with escalating food prices without the benefit of a plan or any clear strategies. Without a battle plan, you will not win a battle, much less a war. This type of shopper simply accepts whatever price they have to pay, and goes right along spending countless thousands of dollars that could be saved with a little effort and some planning.

In this book, you will learn my battle plan for saving hundreds of dollars every year on grocery shopping, which will mostly be done on a week-to-week basis.

You will become a saver shopper who will eat a lot better for a whole lot less. Your mind will be clear when you are shopping, and you will be organized and in complete control. In short, you will become absolutely confident in every area of your food shopping.

Whether you shop for ten people or only one, you will save in proportion to the amount you buy, but you will save every time you shop. When you shop in accordance with the principles in this book, you will always get the very best from every dollar spent, and make your money count. You will not spend extra when you don't have to. You will become an *elite shopper*. You might look the same on the outside, but you will be a far better shopper than you ever imagined possible.

Remember, this book teaches you about grocery shopping, but you can expand your savings in other non-grocery stores to save even more money on staple goods and services. I encourage you to apply what you learn here about this subject to other areas, adding your own knowledge to what I teach. In doing this, you will become increasingly confident and comfortable, and achieve even greater savings.

OVERVIEW

As you read about the principles I recommend in this book, do not become overwhelmed by what it takes to become an *elite grocery shopper*. We will work on all the principles one by one.Never be in a rush while shopping, or doing anything to meet your money-saving goals. There are over 52 opportunities to practice in just one year. In any worthy endeavor, repetition always brings enhanced skill to that particular endeavor. As you practice, you will need to go no further than your record keeping to see the results we are looking for. Those results are eating well and saving money while doing so.

Never let discouragement creep in, because not every week is the same. Some weeks you will make better savings, and other weeks not as much but, when you look back after some time, you will see that your hard work has not been in vain. Remember, we are in competition with rising food prices and the grocery stores. They want to make money, and we want to save ours. My method has been perfected over many years, and it will do for you what it has done for my family and me.

Working these principles into your shopping routine is the key to success. Every principle will become automatic in thinking and execution.

Prices in the marketplace fluctuate all the time, up and down from a set price to a sale price. We must keep a careful eye on these fluctuations, to keep abreast of the constant upward price movement that occurs because of inflation.

By doing this, we will keep abreast of the actual price of a product before any discounts are applied to it. So we get an accurate view of the actual saving right now, and not six to nine months ago. Your knowledge of these price increases is the key to recognizing your savings clearly.

Remember, once a base price has been adjusted upward for inflation, it is not going to come down again.

CHAPTER 1
THE COST OF EATING

We will now look at the price fluctuation of different products. Staple items, like canned goods, boxed goods, laundry soaps and related products, fluctuate in price much less. You will see that, when watched closely, there is a steady upward price movement but at a slow pace. These gradual price increases allow us to get a better understanding of the sales and special pricing put onto these items. You will be able to see more easily the saving you will make on a weekly basis.

Produce

Produce, being fruits and vegetables, is governed in price by the weather, supply and demand, availability and other factors. At the time of writing, produce pricing is going up extremely fast. Most of the time, the sales and specials on produce are not as good and there are not as many. Produce items fluctuate in price according to the season, so keep track of when you get the lower pricing on the produce you buy regularly. You will need to use flexibility here. Know what is good pricing and what is not! Savings in the other areas of the grocery store will absorb some of these escalating prices and still allow you to save plenty. Fruits and vegetables will fluctuate the most, but the rest of your food shopping will give you a pretty clear view of your money-saving opportunities.

Meat, seafood

You will need to learn about your cuts of meat and seafood to understand what is going on in this area. I'll tell you a few things that you need to know.

Not every cut of meat is the same, so you need to brush up on the various different cuts and their basic prices. Do most of your research on the types of meat and cuts you buy on a regular basis. As you watch the prices, you will often find that a cheaper cut is glamorized as a real saving when in fact the sale price could be a dollar more than its regular price three months ago. *Remember, the grocery stores are counting on your having a bad memory.*

You will discover the better cuts of meat, and they will be overpriced half the time. We will outsmart the stores by knowing what a good price is, using our learned flexibility in the selection of that particular week's buys.

You will notice if the carefully-watched prices of the same cut fluctuate from week to week. When we take advantage of "buy one, get one free" sales, this insulates us against price hikes for many weeks until another buying opportunity comes up.

Frozen foods

There is much going on in the frozen food department. Sales abound, saving abounds, and price increases and fluctuations are held to a minimum.

When it comes to buying easy, fast lunches and dinners that you can store for a time, this is the place to look. Nothing can replace a home-cooked meal, but with the number of healthy frozen meals, you will be able to find great savings here. Frozen vegetables are also a fairly-priced commodity, but the quantity you get for the price shows how you pay for their preparation. You will always find good coupon and sale values with frozen foods, company competing against company, and you are right there exercising your right to save.

Learn how to take advantage of a good sale price! One example involves a very good bagged frozen meal. The meal per bag is usually overpriced in my estimate, but of high quality. Approximately every 60 days, the store puts these items on sale for a saving of three dollars a bag, and I stock up at that time only.

On top of that saving, every three months I find one-dollar coupons (going on the internet you can find them even more often). So, if I have some coupons for these items, I use them to leverage the price down even further. All in all, coupons or not, I *wait the company out* and reap savings by buying these items only when they are on sale. Get excited about the game of saving money in the grocery store! Be enthusiastic and your savings will increase.

CHAPTER 2
FLEXIBILTY

Variety is another way you'll be a cut above your fellow shoppers. Always buy according to what's on sale that week! You are always thinking about putting dinners together, so why not incorporate the savings principles into this? Before long, you'll be thinking something like this: Oh, I can save this much on this meat product, and if I put these two side dishes with it, between them I'm feeding my family for this much. Most of the time, once the calculating is done, you are eating well for much less than if you simply chose meals with no regards for price. It's fun to save in this savvy way.

Shopping like this saves you money, especially when your usual meat does not go on sale for several weeks. We just make an alternate plan, and keep right on saving and eating well. The more you are flexible and open to eating a wide range of different foods, the more you can take advantage of the grocery store.

Specific buying

Let's focus on specific buying. I have found that, if you only target your sale items in your secondary store and stick to your shopping list closely, as a principle you save *more* money. This is because, when you go into the grocery store, you always find unadvertised items on sale. If you change your specific plan of what you are going to purchase, you start to lose your focus and needlessly buy other items that you do not need at the time. You can always come across a better deal that stands out and is a good opportunity to buy, so go ahead and purchase that item. But the principle still stands: Target specific items, purchase them and then leave the store!

Store flexibility

An important concept for big savings in the grocery store is flexibility. Everybody has their favorite store, the one where you know every square inch and half the personnel. That one store will save you money but, if one store saves you a certain amount, then two stores will save you more, often much more.

You must rid yourself of that one-store mentality and shop in at least two stores on a weekly basis. I'm not saying every single week, but most of the time. Sometimes there is not enough saving to make it worth going to the secondary store, but more often than not there are big savings there that your favorite store does not have. Combine them, and your savings add up quickly.

When shopping in your secondary store, after reading the sales flyer you might see that there are only three or four items you consider worthy of purchase. When that situation arises, always make the effort to stop in and make those purchases! In doing this, you are resisting getting lazy, and showing consistency in the principle of two-store shopping. You will save money, whether a lot or little, and it all adds up in the year-end totals.

If, by chance, you cannot find anything worthy of the extra stop, then go ahead and use your main store only. There is no point in shopping in two stores if the saving is not worth the time and effort. Approximately 80 % of the time, you will use two stores.

Stores are always competing for business. They time their sales to be one step ahead of the competition, and that is why there is a multitude of sales every week. Grocery wholesalers always offer discounts to stores on particular products, and the stores pass these on to the consumer to various degrees.

Why do you need to know this? The more you know about every aspect of grocery retailing, the more that knowledge will help you in dealing with grocery stores. Being aware of their timing, and getting a feel for how they operate, gives you an edge. Put your mind to work on this subject and, little by little, your overall savings will grow!

There is another thing that could prevent you from achieving your goal of being a top saver in the grocery-shopping arena. This is your attitude! You cannot allow the different requirements the stores have stop you from saving in that particular store because you consider it unacceptable. You can't let in the pride factor, which says, I don't think that's right or fair, so I'm not going to shop there. Drop this attitude, or else you'll drop your overall savings.

Your only attitude must be, I will do whatever it takes to shop there and save money there. Most of the time, it is nothing more than an identification card or some minor requirement like that. The elite grocery shopper does whatever it takes to save, so don't allow fussy likes or dislikes to keep you from your goal.

Brand flexibility

We all like certain brands of the things we buy all the time. But sometimes we are hesitant to try something new, even if it is going to save us money. We know what our brand tastes like; the other brand is a mystery. But flexibility in this area, willingness to try different brands of identical items,is another way to increase overall savings.

There are many savings to be had if we practice not getting stuck on one brand of product. There are some products that, once found, should not be compromised on, but there are many others that can and should be bought flexibly. After practicing buying different brands, your experience of what is good and what is bad or undesirable will grow, and your decision making with future purchases will be enhanced, thus improving your overall savings. This practice, once mastered, is one more reason you will be one of the elite in the grocery-shopping arena. So start experimenting with different products, and your savings will accelerate!

CHAPTER 3
COUPONS

The definition of a coupon is this: a discount voucher presented at purchase, in essence, *free money*!

There are many types of coupons, but we will talk about grocery coupons, and how to find and use them. The easiest place to find coupons is in your newspaper, usually the Sunday papers. Then there are USPS mailings and of course the Internet. Make sure the stores that you shop in accept Internet coupons, because some do not.

When cutting coupons, remember that more is better. Half of your coupons will probably expire before use, but it is always better to have too many than be caught without one when you could really use it. As a general rule, you can expect to save 20–25 % of your total expenditure per visit to the store.

Coupons used to save you as much as 40–50 % but, with the advent of special savings, two-for-one specials and various other special store sales, this is now lower. Coupons are a big part of a successful, money-saving way of shopping for life's essential goods, so always use them!

Coupons can save you considerably, but they should not be abused. Buying an item when you do not have a good coupon will lead you into greediness and is actually less saving. Do not be afraid to put the coupons away if there is a better buying opportunity and the one you thought was good turns out not to be what you expected, when evaluating the sales. This evaluation comes from comparisons of like items at the time of purchase, and might actually save you more money than using the coupons.

Be careful with double-coupon pricing, when a store doubles the face value of a coupon. This can also lead to greed, when you buy too much and waste it, or you buy something where the price has been inflated and not save what you think you're saving. Stores count on your not knowing your pricing well, and so what looks good might not be such a great deal.

Here is an example:
I saw a sale on marinated meat that said, buy one and get one free. I already knew what this meat usually sells for, and I saw that the price was two dollars more per pound. This was still a good deal,

but not what I expected. My potential saving was cut down considerably from my pre-store evaluation. I had two one dollar coupons, and I used them for what is called double coverage savings.

The best way to save with coupons is in this order:

1. Use them on items in a two-for-one sale
2. Use them on items that have sale pricing
3. Use them just to save good money on items you can use

Over the years, I've saved considerable money and you will too if you use coupons habitually. Not every shopping outing is the same, so don't worry about how many or how few coupons you use on any particular outing, just make them a part of your overall plan.

Do not be lazy about using coupons, or finding them! Remember, this is free money that adds up over time, so enjoy using them. Get a good organizer to save your coupons in, with labels for each food category. Keep them organized, and this will save you thought and time.

Check-out line

Before entering the check-out line in the store, organize the coupons you are going to use. Before you unload your groceries from the trolley, hand the coupons to the cashier so you don't forget, and

Watch carefully that the cashier takes them off your bill.

Never be embarrassed to cash your coupons in, never! Take advantage of stores' various sales and price cuts. Don't buy for the sake of buying, outsmart them, use them! You'll amaze yourself with your new ability of not giving any unnecessary money to the grocery stores.

CHAPTER 4
SALES, SPECIALS, CATALOGS

Most sales or specials are only there to get your attention. The grocery store wants to confuse you with the multitude of sale items. But you are not going to allow the store to confuse you. You must inform yourself of the pricing on many items; that way, you'll know if you are going to saving a lot or only a little.

This may sound like a big task but, if you just concentrate, you'll surprise yourself with your mental recall. Always try to recall the special price you once paid for a particular item, and then compare that price with the present-day sale. Remember, the cost of eating is going up along with everything else, so adjust your valuation of the items accordingly.

There are certain times during the yearly cycle when food companies run their discounts, and then it's up to the stores to pass these on to you. Making notes on the timing of different product sales will help keep you informed about upcoming opportunities. Stores also run their own sales often, according to supply and demand. Make the most of these opportunities and run with them from week to week. Looking for sales and specials can be a fun time! This is a time when you are seeking out savings opportunities that save you the bottom line: money!

However, just because something is on sale does not mean you should always buy it! There can be problems with sale items. The price could be inflated to make the sale look like a better deal than it actually is. For example, the grocery store will glamorize a cheaper cut of meat to make it appear to be a great buy. Stores will also do this with less-popular brands and generic products that do not offer the same quality as good brands. *Instead, seek out or wait for sales on better quality items, and eat better for about the same price.*

Sometimes you will see advertisements touting so-called health food and alternative items. It is to your advantage to investigate this further, to see if the ads are really the truth. For example, hormone-free meat costs more than regular meat. You must weigh the extra cost against any health benefit you may get.

The same principle applies with organic fruit and vegetables. Low-fat items are also notorious for price increases; the more fat taken out, the more we pay. Do a little investigation, week by week, year by year, and determine for you and your family if the benefits outweigh the extra cost, and then adjust your buying according to the shopping principles you have already learned.

Remember, retailers put ads in the papers to attract us to items they want to sell. Whether the sales are worthwhile or not is up to you to decide, and not the stores. You need to decide, firstly, is the purchase cost-effective? And, secondly, is it really worth what the store says it is worth? Just because they say it is worth this or that does not mean you are saving any money on it. Your job is to decide whether it is worth what it appears to be.

For example, I went to my secondary (specific buying) store, and when I got to the meat section I found a buy-one-get-one-free sale on a particular cut of roast. First I compared the price with what was listed in the catalog. I found that each roast was about four pounds. For a big family that's a good size, but for a family of three people it is too big. I could not find one roast that was less than four pounds, which told me that the store was making these roasts that size on purpose, so that each roast cost between twelve and seventeen dollars. Even though this was two-for-one, if the number of people in your family is too few to eat that much, you should pass this sale by, and not buy it!

Make your decisions about this sale and then don't think about it anymore about it; just concentrate on the remainder of your list.

Catalogs

The catalogs that stores send to you are just a brief overview of their upcoming sales. You can find a more complete list on the internet sites for each store, but this is not necessary. Always go over the catalog to keep abreast of other sales, even if you are not planning to use them at this time, to get a feel for what they are offering; this is for your information. The better informed you are, the better you will do. So always welcome grocery catalogs, they are another tool that will help you add to your savings totals! Look through them thoroughly with the expectation of finding something that will enhance your savings.

With sales and advertising now shifting toward the healthy side, you will find ads touting organic or low-hormone meat and other health-conscious terms. If you care about these kinds of food, your job is to keep up-to-date on the differences between the good and the not-so-good products, and decide whether you are willing to pay the price difference. Low-fat, organic, low-hormone and such foods always cost more.

I have found that praying over my food, and listening to what God says about it, makes it safer and costs a significant amount less. It is your job to discover differences in prices and decide what you will purchase. Make the decision and then move on, don't dwell on it.

It is a good idea to stay familiar with all the new terms and descriptions the stores use. You do not want to be wondering if this product is better than that other product because you don't understand the description of the product, so do a little homework. This will keep your evaluation process simple.

CHAPTER 5
GROCERY LISTS

You should *always make a grocery list* of at least 80 % of what you will need to buy for a week, or whatever your time frame is in between shopping days. You need to keep your mind clear to make proper decisions, and trying to memorize your list is a big mistake. There will always be some items you don't remember until you are going down the aisles, but the majority should be on the list.

Get to know your stores

You need to memorize most of what is found in each aisle of the store you mainly shop in. This is not too hard and, if you think about it, you'll be surprised at how much you already know; now you just need learn the rest of the aisles. Within a few short months, you will know where the majority of different categories of items is found. This is important, firstly, so that you start at one end of the store and make your way directly to the other end. Secondly, when making your list, you list all the items you need starting with the first aisle in the store, and then all the other rows in the order that you go down them.

Keep practicing this and you will become very good at it. This stops you from going back and forth all over the store. It frees your mind to concentrate on taking full advantage of the sales, coupons etc. that are being offered that week. Frustration in the store only leads to fewer savings on your part.

Sub-list different sections

It is a good idea to list the different areas of the store separately. I list just two: frozen food and fruit and vegetables. Sectioning these off makes reading the list easier and less confusing. Supermarkets can be busier than Grand Central Station, so the less confusion the better.

Use symbols

On your list, for the items you know are on sale, use different symbols corresponding to the sale on the particular item. If it's buy-one-get-one-free, you could use "2 for 1". A coupon could be ©. This makes for an easier shopping session.

Customize your shopping list

It is up to you how your list looks, and I encourage you to use your own wording and symbols. It may be just your needs for the week, but it is also your battle plan for saving. Food prices will keep going up, but your plan will save you many dollars that others will spend needlessly because of unpreparedness.

It is necessary to check the sale catalogs every week; they are limited but you can get a good overview. There will always be some items and sales that you will be interested in. Keep the catalogs handy all week for reference.

CHAPTER 6
RECORD KEEPING

Prices always fluctuate for life's essential goods and services. It is a good idea to keep track of any price fluctuation, in order to know exactly where your hard-earned dollars are going. This is particularly important in the food-buying business. Food prices in the past couple of years have been going up at an accelerated rate, and it is your job to know what price you are paying on a weekly basis. For this, you have to keep records and so will need an accounting-style lined notebook with columns.

The basic way of keeping track of spending is as follows:

1. column 1: date
2. column 2: price
3. column 3: store name
4. column 4: savings without coupons

    5. column 5: savings with coupons.

This way of recording your shopping patterns will show you all aspects of your savings and give you a clear view of what you have saved, where you have shopped and the time of year.

Record keeping is very important because, without it, your memory has to serve the same purpose and it is not as reliable.

Looking back on your record keeping, you can see when you saved more or less, when you were able to use more coupons, and so on. Knowing these trends allows you to seize better savings opportunities and increase the dollar amount you have been saving you and your family. There will be no gray areas about your spending and when it occurred. You must not leave this to memory; the more informed you are, the more you'll save in the future. The time spent in record keeping is short, and the knowledge you obtain from this will make you a more savvy food shopper.

You can expand on this basic record if you like, and include different sales of items, prices, location etc. It is up to you how you want to do it, but basic record keeping is mandatory for the *Elite Grocery Shopper*.

Sup. To Record Keeping

This graph that follows is an example of how you can use record keeping to keep yourself fully informed with regards to your week to week savings through the year. It's important to have Date, Place of Purchase, Amount Paid, Non Coupon Savings, Coupon Savings and Total Savings.

As I have previously stated, your savings, on any particular week, will fluctuate. It is very important to be diligently consistent with record keeping, never missing a week, and in so doing, your expanded results will be magnified before your eyes!

The totals in this following example graph are Real past outings but are not for successive weeks but just to show you how you can make your own record keeping graph.

I encourage you to make your record keeping page according to your likes and dislikes, something your comfortable with. You could also include columns with your #1 store and # 2 store in separate columns.

Most of all, enjoy the process of keeping track of your expanded savings.

Date		$	NAME	ADVAN.		COUPON	
9	9	101.27	Pub.	11.	02		
9	10	22.93	W.D.	10.	54		
9	17	74.52	Pub.	13.	40		
9	18	24.34	W.D.	22.	95	3.	50
9	23	69.50	Pub.	12.	37		
9	24	27.94	W.D	6.	96		
9	30	31.26	W.D	8.	84		
		62.19	Pub.	7.	78	2.	05
10	8	107.62	Pub.	23.	15	3.	50
		13.23	W.D.	5.	79		
10	14	85.54	Pub.	14.	17	5.	85
10	21	98.66	Pub.	27.	42	2.	00
10	22	20.56	W.D.	20.	20		
10	28	71.65	Pub.	25.	64	2.	00
11	12	108.54	Pub.	24.	80		30
11	19	110.87	Pub.	26.	48	8.	25
12	2	53.42	W.D.	36.	73		
		90.75	Pub.	13.	04	1.	20
12	16	86.86	Pub.	20.	38	.	50
12	22	80.06	Pub.	13.	60	3.	10
12	31	57.16	W.D.	23.	19	2.	05
		83.86	Pub.	11.	14	1.	00
1	6	73.48	Pub.	17.	37		
1	27	102.15	Pub.	34.	71		
2	3	118.18	Pub.	21.	56	2.	35

CHAPTER 7
STOCKING UP

A simple thing that squirrels do is first collect their food and then hide it, so that when food gets scarce, they remember where the extra food is and go back to where they hid it and eat what would otherwise be unavailable at that time. God put this idea into their heads to help them stay alive in leaner times.

In much the same way, if you follow this advice you will reap the benefits. At certain times there will be outstanding opportunities to stock up on particular products. Later, when you need them, you can simply take them out of storage, and are able to save dollars over what they presently sell for.

Having places to store products for future use is essential to big savings; do this all the time! Unused cabinets or plastic containers are two ideas for places you could store items.

When stocking up on items, buy them on sale at two-for-one and heavy discounts, thus saving plenty when you don't see them at that price for the next 3–6 months or more. Knowing the shelf life of various products is important; canned goods and some plastic products, for example mayonnaise, can be stored for a considerable time. Beware of boxed and bagged items, whose shelf life is much shorter, and also frozen foods which are good, but having too much could lead to freezer burn.

Watching out for and keeping records of sales, you'll become an expert at predicting the timing of sales of particular items. Some go on sale often, others not so often. The frequent ones you won't have to buy at an inferior price, but can wait for a better pricing opportunity. With others that you don't see on sale as often, you'll stock up to save your money 6-8 months down the track until they are on sale again.

You must know the timing of your consumption of the different products you buy for your family, and don't get greedy. If you buy too much, then you could consume more than usual and lose money. You may also think you are saving but actually losing because of food going bad or stale, freezer burn etc.

It is fun to save money when others don't. It is fun to see with your own eyes all the money you are saving on a weekly basis. Practice saving in an organized way, and always check what stock you have. Having stores creates the opportunity to wait for better sale prices. Practice stocking up a little at first, and then more as you get to know the timing on sales of particular items. Don't worry about the storage space available; just do what you can and it will save you many dollars.

CHAPTER 8
EXAMPLES OF SHOPPING OUTINGS

These examples are taken from some of the shopping days in my recent past. They show the savings that I fully expect anyone to achieve using the principles in this book. I have usually shopped for a family of two adults and one child. You can expect your savings to increase as your spending goes up.

Every week is different in terms of how much you will save. The reason for this is very simple: the grocery stores are not co-operating with you some weeks. But you will still save plenty as long as you put into practice the wisdom you have amassed, and stay consistent in your shopping outings.

As the prices we pay for our food go up, I have found that the competition for customers between stores also increases. This can be seen in the specials and deals they offer the paying public.

You can expect to save hundreds of dollars on coupon savings, and a thousand dollars for two people, two to three thousand for bigger families, in store specials and weekly sales every year.

CHAPTER 9
RECEIPTS

These receipts are shown for example only. They are for both main-store shopping and specific-store shopping.

The main store is where you do the bulk of your shopping, and the specific or secondary store is where you shop for specific sales items *only*.

I am a conservative shopper, and have three people in my family. Your potential savings will depend on:

1. Using all the principles in this book;
2. The kind of shopper you are, conservative or more open;
3. The number of people you shop for.

Some weeks there will be phenomenal savings, and other weeks you'll be squeezing out everything you can from the principles to achieve savings. Over the period of one year, you will save hundreds or thousands over what you do now, and that is you're bottom line.

The blacked-out words are to protect stores' names.

MAIN STORE

```
DIET COCA COLA
 1 @ 10 FOR     10.00        1.00 T F
    Ad Spec Savings  0.50
MOUNTAIN DEW 2LTR             1.49 T F
SPRITE
 1 @ 10 FOR     10.00        1.00 T F
    Ad Spec Savings  0.50
Cashier Confirmed - Age Over 21
NEGRA MODELO 12PK           13.69 T
HUNT'S KETCHUP               1.49   F
HUNT'S KETCHUP               1.49   F
  Promotion                 -1.49   F
    Ad Spec Savings  1.49
8 CONT SOY MK VAN
 1 @  2 FOR      5.00        2.50   F
    Adv Buy Savings  0.59
8 CONT SOY MK VAN
 1 @  2 FOR      5.00        2.50   F
    Adv Buy Savings  0.59
OS LGHT CRANBERRY            3.47 T F
OS LGHT CRANBERRY            3.47 T F
  Promotion                 -3.47 T F
    Ad Spec Savings  3.47
OS LGHT CRANBERRY            3.47 T F
OS LGHT CRANBERRY            3.47 T F
  Promotion                 -3.47 T F
    Ad Spec Savings  3.47
SNUGGLE FAB SOFT             3.89 T
V-8 VEGETABLE JUCE           3.69   F
        HALF & HALF          2.49   F
        HALF & HALF          2.49   F
C/L FRUIT PUNCH              3.99 T F
CLASSIC ROMAINE              2.49   F
BIRDSEYE COB CORN            2.79   F
    Adv Buy Savings  0.40
AUNT/J BTRMLK/PNCK
 1 @  3 FOR      5.00        1.67   F
    Adv Buy Savings  0.32
LONDON BROIL                 8.13   F
    Ad Spec Savings  3.80
BROCCOLI WRAPPED
 1 @  2 FOR      3.00        1.50   F
    Ad Spec Savings  0.69
        FROZEN YGRT          2.89   F
    Adv Buy Savings  0.40
BANANAS
1.92 lb @     0.49/ lb       0.94   F
LC ODF SAN/FE R/BE
 1 @  3 FOR      6.00        2.00   F
    Ad Spec Savings  0.19
LC SPA SESAME STIR
 1 @  3 FOR      6.00        2.00   F
    Ad Spec Savings  0.99
OM DELI TRKY/CHDR
 1 @  2 FOR      5.00        2.50   F
    Ad Spec Savings  0.39
LC CC AS SW/SR CKN
 1 @  3 FOR      6.00        2.00   F
    Ad Spec Savings  0.99
LC SPA STIR FRY


 1 @  3 FOR      6.00        2.00   F
    Ad Spec Savings  0.99
PUBLIX WHOLE FRYER           4.19   F
    Ad Spec Savings  1.26
KEL GO TRTS STRWBY           2.79   F
KRAFT MAC/CHEESE             1.09   F
KRAFT MAC/CHEESE             1.09   F
B/BIRD SWISS ROLLS           1.19   F
ATHENA CANTALOUPE
 1 @  2 FOR      4.00        2.00   F
    Ad Spec Savings  0.99
SMFLD THICK BACON
 1 @  2 FOR      6.00        3.00   F
    Ad Spec Savings  1.79
KG CHERRY BARS               3.39   F
KG RSPBRRY BARS              3.39   F
  Promotion                 -3.39   F
    Ad Spec Savings  3.39
B/BIRD SWISS ROLLS           1.19   F
C/LGHT RSP GRN TEA           3.99 T F
  Promotion                 -3.99 T F
    Ad Spec Savings  3.99
OM DELI HAM/CHDR
 1 @  2 FOR      5.00        2.50   F
    Ad Spec Savings  0.39
KRAFT HND SNK CHOC           1.49   F
BABY RUTH                    2.89 T F
BUTTERFINGER                 2.89 T F
  Promotion                 -2.89 T F
    Ad Spec Savings  2.89
SEATTLES BEST                5.99   F
    Adv Buy Savings  2.00
        FOB YOGURT
 1 @  7 FOR      4.00        0.58   F
     FOB YOG MANGO
 1 @  7 FOR      4.00        0.57   F
     FOB YOGURT
 1 @  7 FOR      4.00        0.57   F
     FOB YOGURT
 1 @  7 FOR      4.00        0.57   F
NAB FIG NEWTON               3.69   F
SNYD BTRMILK RANCH
 1 @  2 FOR      4.00        2.00   F
    Ad Spec Savings  0.89
Vendor Coupon               -0.60   F
Vendor Coupon               -0.75   F
VENDOR COUPON               -1.00   F
Balance Due                118.77
Cash                       120.00
 Sales Tax                   2.27
Change                       1.23

Your Total Savings
Vendor Coupon                2.35
Advertised Special Savings  32.86
Advantage Buy Savings        4.30
Your Savings at             39.51
```

```
DT SUNKIST ORANGE
1 @  3 FOR    4.00         1.34 T F
    Ad Spec Savings  0.15
DT DR PEP CHRY VAN
1 @  3 FOR    4.00         1.33 T F
    Ad Spec Savings  0.15
ARIZONA DT GRN TEA         2.99 T F
MOUNTAIN DEW 2LTR
1 @  3 FOR    4.00         1.33 T F
    Ad Spec Savings  0.15
V-8 VEGETABLE JUCE         3.69   F
WHT GRPFT JUCE             2.79   F
ULT DET HE                 3.49 T
WHOLE MILK                 1.49   F
HALF & HALF                2.45   F
C/LGHT RASPBRY TEA         4.69   F
C/LGHT RASPBRY TEA         4.69   F
Promotion                 -4.69   F
    Ad Spec Savings  4.69
BALSAMIC VINEGAR
1 @  2 FOR    3.00         1.50   F
    Adv Buy Savings  0.69
G S ITALIAN DRESS          3.59   F
CAMP CREAM OF MUSH         1.29   F
CAMP CREAM OF MUSH         1.29   F
LIME AWAY CA RM SP         3.29 T
Vendor Coupon             -0.50   F
SNUGGLE FAB SOFT           3.39 T
    Adv Buy Savings  0.50
ALPO PRIME CUTS            0.99 T
ALPO PRIME CUTS GR         0.99 T
ALPO PR CT BF/STW          0.99 T
Vendor Coupon             -0.99 T
BREY PNUT BTR TRAC         5.29   F
BREYERS FR VANILLA         5.29   F
Promotion                 -5.29   F
    Ad Spec Savings  5.29
JOY LIQ DISH DETG          2.19 T
Vendor Coupon             -0.30   F
PUB SOUR CREAM             1.09   F
CHUCK ROAST BNLS           7.37   F
    Ad Spec Savings  3.28
BLUEBIRD PECAN SPN         0.99   F
    Adv Buy Savings  0.20
ROSETTO CH RAVIOLI
1 @  2 FOR    6.00         3.00   F
    Adv Buy Savings  0.69
FOB YOG GUAVA
1 @  10 FOR   5.00         0.50   F
    Ad Spec Savings  0.07
FOB YOGURT
1 @  10 FOR   5.00         0.50   F
    Ad Spec Savings  0.07
FOB YOG MANGO
1 @  10 FOR   5.00         0.50   F

    Ad Spec Savings  0.07
ROSETTO CH RAVIOLI
1 @  2 FOR    6.00         3.00   F
    Adv Buy Savings  0.69
JD SAUSAGE HOT             2.99   F
MILLSTONE COFFEE           5.99   F
    Adv Buy Savings  2.00
LRGE EGGS                  1.39   F
FE PREMIUM ROMAINE         2.49   F
FE PREMIUM ROMAINE         2.49   F
SMUCKER PB & HONEY         2.39   F
ST FAIR MINI C/DOG         4.69   F
PISTACHIOS                 3.99   F
    Ad Spec Savings  1.50
Vendor Coupon             -1.00   F
POTATOES IDAHO             2.99   F
R/G BRAID CLASSIC          2.49   F
SNYD C/C PRTZ SAND
1 @  2 FOR    6.00         3.00   F
    Adv Buy Savings  0.49
Vendor Coupon             -0.75   F
BANANAS
2.68 lb @    0.49/ lb      1.31   F
NAB VARIETY PACK           5.69   F
NAB SS FIG NEWTON          5.69   F
Promotion                 -5.69   F
    Ad Spec Savings  5.69
KRAFT HND SNK CHOC         1.49   F
BOUNTY S A S PRNT          1.99 T
QUAK INST OATS
1 @  2 FOR    5.00         2.50   F
    Ad Spec Savings  1.29
GM VAR PAK CRL BAR         3.09   F
UNC BEN VEG HRVST          1.67   F
UNC BEN VEG HRVST          1.67   F
Promotion                 -1.67   F
    Ad Spec Savings  1.67
KLEENEX COTTN BATH
1 @  2 FOR    12.00        6.00 T
    Ad Spec Savings  2.29
Vendor Coupon             -0.25   F
Balance Due             -124.17
    Check   Purchase    124.17
    AUTH#: 174531
    Sales Tax              1.98
Change                     0.00

Your Total Savings
Vendor Coupon              3.79
Advertised Special Savings 26.36
Advantage Buy Savings      5.26
Your Savings at           35.41
```

```
A&H LIQ ORCHARD              4.45 T      BROTHER'S WHOLE BN          6.99  F
DIET SPRITE ZERO                           Adv Buy Savings 1.00
1 @  4 FOR    5.00          1.25 T F    STOU BBQ CHICKEN
  Ad Spec Savings 0.14                   1 @  3 FOR    6.00         2.00  F
FANTA ZERO ORANGE                          Ad Spec Savings 0.99
1 @  4 FOR    5.00          1.25 T F    EDYS LIGHT CHOCOL
  Ad Spec Savings 0.14                   1 @  2 FOR    7.00         3.50  F
▬▬▬ULT BLEACH F             1.29 T        Ad Spec Savings 1.79
  Ad Spec Savings 0.38                  BANANAS
OS LT CRAN COCKTL           4.99 T F      2.51 lb @   0.49/ lb      1.23  F
DIET COCA COLA                          FRITO TWST HNY BBQ          2.49  F
1 @  4 FOR    5.00          1.25 T F    FRITO REG CRN CHIP          2.49  F
OS LT CRAN COCKTL           4.99 T F      Promotion                -2.49  F
  Promotion               -4.99 T F       Ad Spec Savings 2.49
  Ad Spec Savings 4.99                  MUELLER PENNE RIGA          0.99  F
▬▬ WHT GRPFT JUCE           2.79   F    MUELLER PENNE RIGA          0.99  F
BUSH ORIG BAKED BN          1.85   F      Promotion                -0.99  F
LOL FF HALF & HALF          2.49   F      Ad Spec Savings 0.99
SILK SOYMILK                3.15   F    STOUFFERS ENTREE
CAPRI LEMNADE 10PK                        1 @  3 FOR    6.00        2.00  F
1 @  4 FOR    7.00          1.75 T F      Ad Spec Savings 0.45
  Ad Spec Savings 0.74                  L/D NUTTY BAR               1.29  F
STARKIST TUNA                           PUB CHOC SUGAR WFR          1.59  F
1 @  2 FOR    4.00          2.00   F    L/D SWISS ROLL              1.19  F
  Ad Spec Savings 1.17                  HUNT SNK PK CH/VAN
BUSH ORIG BAKED BN          1.85   F      1 @  5 FOR    4.00        0.80  F
  Promotion               -1.85   F       Adv Buy Savings 0.19
  Ad Spec Savings 1.85                  HUNT CHC VAR PUDDG
CONT SHRP STIR FRY          5.99   F      1 @  5 FOR    4.00        0.80  F
CONT SHRP STIR FRY          5.99   F       Adv Buy Savings 0.19
  Promotion               -5.99   F    ▬▬ FOB YOG GUAVA
  Ad Spec Savings 5.99                   1 @  7 FOR    4.00         0.58  F
CONT SHRP STIR FRY          5.99   F    ▬▬ FOB YOGURT
SNUGGLE FAB SOFT            2.99 T      1 @  7 FOR    4.00          0.57  F
  Ad Spec Savings 0.90                  SCOTTOWEL MEGA ROL
ART& SPINACH DIP            5.19   F      1 @  3 FOR    4.00        1.34 T
▬▬ X LRGE EGGS              1.39   F      Adv Buy Savings 0.18
CONT SHRP STIR FRY          5.99   F    Balance Due               102.15
  Promotion               -5.99   F      Check    Purchase        102.15
  Ad Spec Savings 5.99                      AUTH#: 144027
▬▬▬ WHOLE CHICK             4.07   F      Sales Tax                  1.34
TOP SIRLOIN STEAK          ·6.06   F      Change                     0.00
  Ad Spec Savings 3.04
PILLSBURY MINI              2.19   F    Your Total Savings
JD S/E&C CROISSANT          6.39   F    Advertised Special Savings 33.17
BAGEL BITES 5 CHS           3.69   F    Advantage Buy Savings       1.54
                                        Your Savings at ▬▬▬        34.71
```

SPECIFIC STORE

```
        LUIGI ITL ICE VRTY RC    3.49 B
        LUIGI ITL ICE VRTY RC    3.49 B
        LUIGI ITL ICE VRTY RC    3.49 B
        F.E. CEASER SUPRME RC    3.49 F
        F.E. AMER SLD/BLND RC    2.99 F
        F.E. HRTS ROMAINE  RC    3.29 F
        VITAMIN E SYN/1000 RC    9.49
        SUNDOWN NIAC       RC    4.69
        1-LB BABY CARROTS  RC    1.99 F
        BE 12 EAR COB CORN RC    3.19 F
        BE 12 EAR COB CORN RC    3.19 F
RC 00027077 BE 12 EAR COB COR    3.19-F
        1-LB BABY CARROTS  RC    1.99 F
RC 00027032 1-LB BABY CARROTS    1.99-F
        BONELESS BREASTS   RC    9.93 F
        BONELESS BREASTS   RC    9.48 F
        BONELESS BREASTS   RC    9.53 F
        CF DIET COKE       RC    1.39 B
        DT CHERRY COKE     RC    1.39 B
RC 00027320 DT CHERRY COKE       1.39-B
        FW MED WHT SHRIMP  RC    7.99 F
        FW MED WHT SHRIMP  RC    7.99 F
        BAY SCALLOPS       RC    5.99 F
RC 00032042 BAY SCALLO (3.99)    2.00-F
        STRKST TUNA        RC     .79 F
        STRKST TUNA        RC     .79 F
        STRKST TUNA        RC     .79 F
        EDGE BON S-MOIST         2.99 T
VERIFIED BY CASHIER
        NEGRO MODELA BEER        7.49 T
     2 @ 3.49
RC 00027037 LUIGI ITL ICE VRT    6.98-B
RC 00027119 F.E. AMER SLD/BLN    2.99-F
RC 00027119 F.E. HRTS ROMAINE    3.29-F
     2 @ 9.48 OR 9.53
RC 00027002 BONELESS BREASTS    19.01-F
RC 00027048 FW MED WHT SHRIMP    7.99-F
     2 @ .79
RC 00028061 STRKST TUNA          1.58-F
     **** TAX     .93 TOT        61.84

MC     SCANN  OUPON              1.00-
     **** TAX     .93 TOT        60.84

VF     PERSONAL CHECK            60.84


TOTAL NUMBER OF ITEMS SOLD = 25
4/09/05  1:52 PM 0308 05 0043 140

         SAVINGS           50.41
MANUF. COUPON SAVINGS       1.00
```

You Saved $51.41

```
            LUIGI ITL ICE VRTY RC      3.49 B
            LUIGI ITL ICE VRTY RC      3.49 B
RC 00030939 LUIGI ITL ICE VRTY         3.49-B
            IMITATION CRAB MT. RC       3.99 F
            IMITATION CRAB MT. RC       3.99 F
RC 00030579 IMITATION CRAB MT.         3.99-F
            SILK VAN. SOYMILK   RC      3.19 F
RC 00032091 SILK VAN. (2.50)            .69-F
            SILK VAN. SOYMILK   RC      3.19 F
RC 00032091 SILK VAN. (2.50)            .69-F
            WD APPLE JUICE PLS RC       1.79 F
RC 00032089 WD APPLE J (1.50)S          .29-F
            V8 VEG JUICE PET.          3.59 F
            WD BTR FLAVOR SYRP         1.69 F
            NAB CHOC GRAHAMS    RC      3.49 F
            NAB CINNAMON GRAHM RC       3.49 F
RC 00027610 NAB CINNAMON GRAHM         3.49-F
            SNO BOL L/BOWL CLN         2.18 T
            BF EYE RND STK      RC      6.08 F
            BF EYE RND STK      RC      6.18 F
RC 00030564 BF EYE RND STK             6.08-F
            CRYO WHOLE FRYER    RC      5.57 F
            CRYO WHOLE FRYER    RC      5.51 F
RC 00030542 CRYO WHOLE FRYER           5.51-F
            M/R 5" PEP PIZZA    RC      2.99 F
            M/R 5" PEP PIZZA    RC      2.99 F
RC 00030612 M/R 5" PEP PIZZA           2.99-F
            HORMEL B/L BACON    RC      4.99 F
            HORMEL LS BACON     RC      4.99 F
RC 00030599 HORMEL LS BACON            4.99-F
            NEW ENG COFFEE BR   RC      5.39 F
            NEW ENG CFFEE COL   RC      5.39 F
RC 00027835 NEW ENG CFFEE COL          5.39-F
            WD AA BATTERIES     RC      4.99 T
            WD AAA BATTERIES    RC      4.99 T
            WD LARGE EGGS               .99 F
   1.56 lb @ 3.99 /lb
WT          FRESH ASPARAGUS     RC      6.22 F
   1.56 lb @ .99 /lb = 1.54
RC 00031427 FRESH ASPARAGUS            4.68-F
RC 00028126 WD AAA BATTERIES           4.99-T
       **** TAX      .64  TOT         58.21

MC          SCANNED COUPON              .50-
RC          FREE WD LARGE EGGS          .99-F
RC          FREE WD APPLE JCE.         1.50-F
RC          FREE WD SYRUP CPN          1.69-F
MC          SCANNED COUPON              .35-F
       **** TAX      .64  TOT         53.18

VF          PERSONAL CHECK            53.18


TOTAL NUMBER OF ITEMS SOLD = 26
6/03/06 12:22 PM 0308 06 0042 125

            SAVINGS           51.45
MANUF. COUPON SAVINGS          .85

You Saved   $52.30
```

```
        EDYS LT PNTBTR CUP RC    5.49 F
        ED LIT RASP CHIP   RC    5.49 F
        W/W SILK V.VANILLA RC    3.19 F
        BF T/RND LNDR BRL  RC    7.93 F
        BF T/RND LNDR BRL  RC    7.83 F
        M/R 5" PEP PIZZA   RC    2.99 F
        M/R 5" PEP PIZZA   RC    2.99 F
    6 @ 2/1.29
        YELLOW CORN        RC    3.87 F
    SAVED 5.13  ON SPECIAL REWARD ITEM
    ███████ CUSTOMER          420XXXX8790

RC 00030044 M/R 5" PEP (.20)      .45-F
RC 00030044 YELLOW CORN (.20)     .44-F
RC 00030044 M/R 5" PEP (.20)      .45-F
RC 00030044 YELLOW CORN (.20)     .44-F
RC 00030044 M/R 5" PEP (.20)      .45-F
RC 00030044 YELLOW CORN (.20)     .44-F
RC 00031647 M/R 5" PEP PIZZA     2.99-F
RC 00032091 W/W SILK V (2.50)A    .69-F
RC 00028712 ED LIT RASP CHIP     5.49-F
        MUELLERS SPAGHETTI RC     .99 F
        MUELLERS SPAGHETTI RC     .99 F
RC 00028811 MUELLERS SPAGHETTI    .99-F
        WD CHS INST GRITS  RC    1.99 F
RC 00032089 WD CHS INS (1.50)     .49-F
        FLNDRS ANGS BURGER RC    7.99 F
        FLNDRS ANGS BURGER RC    7.99 F
RC 00031659 FLNDRS ANGS BURGER   7.99-F
RC 00031407 BF T/RND LNDR BRL    7.83-F
    **** TAX      .00 TOT      30.59

VF      PERSONAL CHECK           30.59


    TOTAL NUMBER OF ITEMS SOLD = 18
    5/07/06  1:14 PM 0308 03 0119 135

    ███████ SAVINGS          29.14
    SPECIAL REWARD SAVINGS    5.13
```

You Saved $34.27

```
              GRHT SHRIMP MEAL           4.99 F
      SAVED 1.00  ON SPECIAL        ITEM
              FW 31/40 WHT SHRMP RC   8.99 F
              FW 31/40 WHT SHRMP RC   8.99 F
      RC 4501 FW 31/40 WHT SHRMP      8.99-F
              PORK LOIN 1/5 SLI  RC  12.67 F
      RC 5985 PORK LOIN 1/5 SLI       5.78-F
              BF LN SRLN STK BNL RC  23.00 F
      RC 5087 BF LN SRLN STK BNL      9.21-F
              KRAFT 6PK MAC/CHSE RC   2.79 F
        1 @ 3/5.00
              DM L/S MAND ORANGE RC   1.67 F
      SAVED .33  ON SPECIAL REWARD ITEM
      RC 4877 DM L/S MAND ORA (1.66)  .01-F
        1 @ 3/5.00
              DM L/S MAND ORANGE RC   1.67 F
      SAVED .33  ON SPECIAL REWARD ITEM
              HMSTYL MESQUT BRST RC   6.99 F
      RC 4634 HMSTYL MESQUT BRST      1.00-F
              YELLOW AMER CHEESE RC   2.07 F
      RC 4653 YELLOW AMER CHEESE       .26-F
              S.B. 18 CT. EGGS        2.29 F
              2# C/S STRWBERRIES RC   5.49 F
      RC 4334 2# C/S STRWBERR (2.99)  2.50-F
              MAHATMA BR/C             .99 F
              MAHATMA BR/C             .99 F
      18.59   CUCUMBERS          RC    .59 F
      RC 4572 CUCUMBERS          (.50  .09-F
              ITALIAN BREAD      RC    .99 F
        1.81 lb @ .49 /lb
      WT      YELLOW BANANAS     RC    .89 F
        1.81 lb @ .39 /lb = .71
      RC 4565 YELLOW BANANAS           .18-F
        **** TAX        .00 TOT      58.04

      RC      FREE ITLN BRED CPN       .99-F
        **** TAX        .00 TOT      57.05


              CASH                   70.00

              CHANGE                 12.95

      TOTAL NUMBER OF ITEMS SOLD =  17
      4/17/04  2:11 PM 0308 01 0134 125


                    SAVINGS          29.01
                    SAVINGS           1.66
      TOTAL SAVINGS                  30.67
```

```
          2LT DIET PEPSI     RC     1.45 B
RC 00027422 2LT DIET P (1.00)       .45-B
          DT MUG ROOT BEER   RC     1.45 B
RC 00027422 DT MUG ROO (1.00)       .45-B
          DIET SIERRA MIST   RC     1.45 B
RC 00027422 DIET SIERR (1.00)       .45-B
          DT CHERRY PEPSI 2L RC     1.45 B
RC 00027422 DT CHERRY  (1.00)       .45-B
          JET-PUFF MINI MSHM        1.99 B
          PILLSBURY H/S WFFL        2.39 F
          PILLS DNKBLE PNCK         2.69 F
          TRISCUIT ROSEMARY         2.99 F
          ONCOR CHICKN PARM  RC     3.99 F
RC 00032092 ONCOR CHIC (3.00)       .99-F
          ONCOR CHICKN PARM  RC     3.99 F
RC 00032092 ONCOR CHIC (3.00)       .99-F
          CRYO WHOLE FRYER   RC     5.44 F
          CRYO WHOLE FRYER   RC     4.91 F
RC 00027921 CRYO WHOLE FRYER        4.91-F
          FW MED WHT SHRIMP  RC     6.99 F
SAVED 1.00  ON SPECIAL REWARD ITEM
          FW MED WHT SHRIMP  RC     6.99 F
SAVED 1.00  ON SPECIAL REWARD ITEM
RC 00027756 FW MED WHT SHRIMP       6.99-F
          FW MED WHT SHRIMP  RC     6.99 F
SAVED 1.00  ON SPECIAL REWARD ITEM
          FW MED WHT SHRIMP  RC     6.99 F
SAVED 1.00  ON SPECIAL REWARD ITEM
RC 00027756 FW MED WHT SHRIMP       6.99-F
          IMITATION CRAB MT. RC     3.99 F
          IMITATION CRAB MT. RC     3.99 F
RC 00027758 IMITATION CRAB MT       3.99-F
          DOLE CLSSC ROMAINE        2.69 F
          SLIM JIM           RC     1.29 F
RC 00027631 SLIM JIM   (1.00)       .29-F
          SLIM JIM           RC     1.29 F
RC 00027631 SLIM JIM   (1.00)       .29-F
          DOLE CLSSC ROMAINE        2.69 F
          SEATTLES B.GND CFE RC     7.69 F
RC 00032047 SEATTLES B (5.99)       1.70-F
2.26 lb @ .49 /lb
WT        TURNING BANANAS    RC     1.11 F
2.26 lb @ .39 /lb = .88
RC 00027551 TURNING BANANAS         .23-F
          LOL PRE/YELLOW     RC     5.14 F
RC 00027424 LOL PRE/YELLOW          1.03-F
          SEATTLES BB B/F CF RC     7.69 F
RC 00032047 SEATTLES B (5.99)       1.70-F
          LD HONEY BUN              1.29 F
          HILTON PAC OYSTERS RC     4.49 F
RC 00032042 HILTON PAC (3.99)       .50-F
     **** TAX       .36  TOT       73.46

MC    SCANNED COUPON              .35-F
     **** TAX       .36  TOT       73.11

VF    PERSONAL CHECK              73.11


TOTAL NUMBER OF ITEMS SOLD = 28
1/21/06  2:31 PM 0308 03 0158 129

          SAVINGS            32.40
MANUF. COUPON SAVINGS          .35
SPECIAL       SAVINGS         4.00

You Saved  $36.75
```

www.ingramcontent.com/pod-product-compliance
Lightning Source LLC
Chambersburg PA
CBHW030010190526
45157CB00015B/2176